DELANEY
STREET
PRESS

Get Well Soon...
We Need You

Get Well Soon...
We Need You

Eight Common-Sense Principles for Hastening Your Healing

Dr. Criswell Freeman

DELANEY STREET PRESS
Nashville, TN: (800) 256-8584

ISBN 1-58334-065-3

The ideas expressed in this book are not, in all cases, exact quotations, as some have been edited for clarity and brevity. In all cases, the author has attempted to maintain the speaker's original intent. In some cases, material for this book was obtained from secondary sources, primarily print media. While every effort was made to ensure the accuracy of these sources, the accuracy cannot be guaranteed. For additions, deletions, corrections or clarifications in future editions of this text, please write DELANEY STREET PRESS.

Printed in the United States of America

2 3 4 5 6 7 8 9 10 • 00 01 02 03 04 05 06

Cover Design by Bart Dawson
Layout by Swan Lake Communications,
Jackson, Mississippi

ACKNOWLEDGMENTS

The author gratefully acknowledges the helpful support of Angela Beasley Freeman, Dick and Mary Freeman, Mary Susan Freeman, Jim Gallery, and the entire team of professionals at DELANEY STREET PRESS and WALNUT GROVE PRESS.

Dedicated to the Memory of
Wayne Oates, and to
His Healing Message
Which Lives On

Table of Contents

The chief use
of a temporary
sickness is to
remind us of
the value
of health.

RALPH WALDO EMERSON

Introduction

Because you're reading a book with the words "Get Well" in its title, you're probably feeling under the weather. If so, this book is designed to lift your spirits and, by doing so, speed your recovery.

This little quotation book is organized into eight chapters, each containing a common-sense principle for getting well sooner. These eight time-tested principles are neither novel nor difficult to comprehend, but they *are* profoundly important. The eight great ideas summarized on the pages of this text can have a direct impact on the speed at which you recover your health.

Sickness is, at best, an extreme inconvenience; the sooner you get well, the better. So do yourself a favor by heeding the following advice.

Your body will thank you.

PRINCIPLE 1

Keep Your Spirits Up

When you're not feeling up to par, it's easy to become discouraged. Your sickness has a way of making your entire world seem gray, while pessimism tends to color your thoughts. But be warned: the sick bed is no place for negative thinkers!

If you sincerely wish to hasten your healing, it's up to you and you alone to observe the first principle of getting well by keeping your spirits up.

Your doctor is working to heal you; your medicine is doing its part; your body is hard at work healing itself. It's your responsibility to enlist your mind in the healing process by becoming a positive patient.

Optimism is a choice: choose it. And while you're at it, consider the quotations that follow.

The optimism of a healthy
mind is indefatigable.
Margery Allingham

The fact that the mind
rules the body is the most
fundamental fact which
we know about the
process of life.
Franz Alexander

It is not possible to heal
the body without engaging
the mind's support.
Meir Schneider

Man is what he believes.
Anton Chekhov

If you constantly think
of illness, you will become ill;
if you believe yourself to be
beautiful, you become so.
Shakti Gawain

If you keep on saying
things are going to be bad,
you have a good chance
of becoming a prophet.
Isaac Bashevis Singer

A merry heart does
  good like a medicine:
  but a broken spirit
  dries the bones.

Proverbs 17:22

Mirth is God's medicine.
  Everybody ought
  to bathe in it.

Henry Ward Beecher

The joy of the mind is
the measure of its strength.

Ninon de Lenclos

The best of healers is good cheer.

PINDAR

Worry and anxiety
   are sand in the machinery
   of life; faith is the oil.
                        E. Stanley Jones

Faith can put a candle in the
         darkest night.
                        Margaret Sangster

Faith is an activity.
   It is something that has
      to be applied.
                        Corrie ten Boom

Faith is not believing that God can, but that God will!

ABRAHAM LINCOLN

Perpetual optimism
is a force multiplier.
Colin Powell

Seeds of faith are always
within us; sometimes it takes
a crisis to nourish and
encourage their growth.
Susan L. Taylor

The body manifests
what the mind harbors.
Jerry Augustine

You can promote your healing by your thinking.

JAMES E. SWEENY

Since the human
body tends to move
in the direction of
its expectations,
it's important
to know that
positive attitudes
are a part
of treatment.

NORMAN COUSINS

Change your thoughts and
you change your world.
Norman Vincent Peale

The happiness of your life
depends on the quality
of your thoughts.
Marcus Aurelius Antoninus

The best part of health
is a fine disposition.
Ralph Waldo Emerson

Sometimes it's more important
to know what kind of patient has a
disease than what kind of disease
the patient has.

William Osler

One's confidence, or lack of it,
in the prospects of recovery from
serious illness affects the
chemistry of the body.

Norman Cousins

Hope is patience
with the lamp lit.

Tertullian

No hope, no action.

Peter Levi

There is no medicine like hope.
O. S. Marden

All human wisdom can be
summed up in two words:
wait and hope.
Alexandre Dumas

Exceptional patients
are self-reliant and seek
solutions rather than
lapsing into depression.
Bernie Siegel, M.D.

If you have an illness,
decide to be well.
Mike Samuels, M.D.

The sound body is
the product of a
sound mind.
George Bernard Shaw

PRINCIPLE 2

Take an Active Role In Your Healing

Simply put, it's up to you to assume the ultimate responsibility for your quick return to health.

Of course, your doctor has a crucial role to play, as do other members of the healing professions. But you, as a savvy patient, are wise to assume responsibility and control over your treatment.

After all, it's your body, and *nobody* has more at stake than you.

There is a future
that makes itself
and a future that
you make. The real
future is composed
of both.

ALAIN

The healthy, the strong ⅄
individual, is the one who
asks for help when he needs it,
whether he has an abscess on
his knee or in his soul.

Rona Barrett

Healing is a matter of time,
but it is sometimes a matter
of opportunity.

Hippocrates

Become an expert in
your own condition.

Tom Ferguson, M.D.

I never worry about action
but only about inaction.
Winston Churchill

We must not sit down
and wait for miracles.
We must be up and going!
John Eliot

Every noble act was
at first impossible.
Thomas Carlyle

It is well to think well.
It is divine to act well.

Horace Mann

All the lovely sentiments
in the world weigh less than
a single lovely action.

James Russell Lowell

Begin to weave, and God
will provide the thread.

German Proverb

For purposes of action,
nothing is more useful than
narrowness of thought
combined with energy of will.

Henri Frederic Amiel

When you come to a
roadblock, take a detour. ✛

Mary Kay Ash

When you come to a fork ✝
in the road, take it.

Yogi Berra

Talk that does not end in
any kind of action is better
suppressed altogether.

Thomas Carlyle

Action is the antidote
to despair.

Joan Baez

Every action of our lives
touches on some chord that
will vibrate in eternity.

Edwin Hubbel Chapin

A sharing of responsibility with one's physician is in the best interest of both physician and patient.

NORMAN COUSINS

We will either find a way or we will make one.

HANNIBAL

Act as if it were
impossible to fail.
Dorthea Brand

Trust in God
and do something.
Mary Lyon

God helps them
who help themselves.
Ben Franklin

Principle 3

Rest

Sickness is the body's way of asking you to slow down while it does its work. Your job, simply put, is to comply.

As your body works overtime to heal itself, you must do your part by preserving —not squandering— energy.

So if your doctor advises you to slow down, listen to her. Let your body work while you rest. There will be plenty of time to busy yourself with other things after you've regained your strength and your health.

Rest has cured
more people than
all the medicine
in the world.

HAROLD J. REILLY

Never hurry; take plenty
of exercise, always be cheerful,
and take all the sleep you
need, and you may expect
to be well.

James Freeman Clarke

He that can take rest is
greater than he that
can take cities.

Ben Franklin

God authorizes us to take
that rest and refreshment
which are necessary to
keep up the strength
of mind and body.

St. John Baptiste de la Salle

Periods of wholesome laziness will wonderfully tone up the mind and body.

GRANVILLE KLEISER

Sleep is the golden chain that ties health and our bodies together.

THOMAS DEKKER

D ays of respite
    are golden days.
                    Robert South

T ake rest; a field that has
rested gives a bountiful crop.
                    Ovid

T o recreate strength, rest.
                    G. Simmons

Rest is a fine medicine.

THOMAS CARLYLE

Rest and be thankful.

WILLIAM WORDSWORTH

PRINCIPLE 4

Cultivate Healthy Habits

Life is a gift — health, on the other hand, must be earned. We earn good health by cultivating healthy habits.

During times of poor health, we may have cause to reevaluate our habits and recommit ourselves to more sensible life-styles.

If your illness has served as a wake-up call that has opened your eyes to the many benefits of good health, congratulations. A healthy lifestyle will enhance your enjoyment of every precious day. And besides, healthy habits are a tangible way of saying "thank you" to the Giver of that priceless gift: life.

The second half of a man's
life is made up of the habits
he acquired during
the first half.

Dostoyevsky

The chains of habit are too
weak to be felt until they are
too strong to be broken.

Samuel Johnson

Make good habits,
and they will make you.

Parks Cousins

Fitness: If it came in a bottle, everybody would have good health.

CHER

The ingredients of health
  and long life are great
  temperance, open air,
easy labor, and little care.

Philip Sidney

To ensure good health:
  Eat lightly, breathe deeply,
  live moderately, cultivate
cheerfulness, and maintain
  an interest in life.

William Louden

The regular and temperate
  life is little affected by
  disorders and mishaps.

Cornaro

Those who do not find time for exercise will have to find time for illness.

EARL OF DERBY

Health is better than wealth.

ENGLISH PROVERB

True enjoyment comes
from activity of the mind
and exercise of the body;
the two are ever united.

Humbolt

The joy of feeling physically
fit is reflected in a clearer
and more useful mind.

Edgar Watson Howe

A careful physician must
investigate not only the malady
of the man he wishes to cure, but
also the habits of the patient.

Marcus Tullius Cicero

Better keep
yourself clean
and bright. You are
the window through
which you must
see the world.

GEORGE BERNARD SHAW

Health is so necessary to all the duties, as well as the pleasures of life, that the crime of squandering it is equal to the folly.

SAMUEL JOHNSON

To preserve health is a moral duty.

SAMUEL JOHNSON

PRINCIPLE 5

Never Give In

On October 29, 1941, Winston Churchill spoke to a group of students and faculty at Harrow School. Churchill advised, "Never give in. Never give in. Never, never, never — in nothing great or small, large or petty — never give in except to conviction of honor and good sense." His words, delivered during the dark days of World War II, apply equally well today for those who face illness.

In sickness, as in war, victory belongs to those who persevere. So even if you're feeling tired, out of sorts, hopeless, or confused, never, never give in. Keep fighting, because in battle and in life, victory belongs to those who keep battling.

Nothing in the world can take the place of persistence. Talent will not .... Genius will not.... Education will not.... Persistence and determination alone are omnipotent.

CALVIN COOLIDGE

Drugs are not always necessary. Belief in recovery always is.

NORMAN COUSINS

Diligence overcomes
difficulties; sloth makes them.
Ben Franklin

Failure is the path of
least persistence.
Old-Time Saying

There is no chance,
no destiny, no fate
that can hinder or control
the firm resolve of
a determined soul.
Ella Wheeler Wilcox

Amen

W hen you get into a tight
place and everything goes
against you, never give up, for
that is just the place and time
that the tide will turn.

Harriet Beecher Stowe

P erhaps perseverance has
been the radical principle of
every truly great character.

John Foster

P atience and diligence, X
like faith, move mountains.

William Penn

The greatest and most sublime power is often simple patience.

Horace Bushnell

Genius is eternal patience.

Michelangelo

Patient waiting is often the highest way of doing God's will.

Collier

To do nothing is sometimes a good remedy.

HIPPOCRATES

God is with those
who patiently persevere.
Arabian Proverb

Courage and perseverance
have a magical talisman,
before which difficulties
and obstacles vanish
into thin air.
John Quincy Adams

You do what you can
for as long as you can,
and when you finally can't,
you do the next best thing.
You back up, but you
don't give up.
Chuck Yeager

This is no time for ease and comfort. This is the time to dare and endure.

WINSTON CHURCHILL

As long as the day lasts,
let's give it all we've got.
David McKay

The word impossible
is not in my dictionary.
Napoleon Bonaparte

True miracles are created by
men when they use the
courage and intelligence that
God gave them.
Jean Anouilh

Courage is the first of
human qualities because
it is the quality which
guarantees all the others.

Winston Churchill

Courage is fear that has
said its prayers.

Dorothy Bernard

Facing it — always facing
it — that's the way to
get through.

Joseph Conrad

Fear corrupts.

John Steinbeck

Keep your fears to yourself,
but share your courage.
Robert Louis Stevenson

Seeds of faith are always
within us; sometimes it
takes a crisis to nourish and
encourage their growth.
Susan L. Taylor

Get Well Soon...We Need You

Fortune favors the brave.

TERENCE

God grant me
the serenity to
accept the things
I cannot change;
the courage to
change the things
I can; and the
wisdom to know
the difference.

REINHOLD NIEBUHR

PRINCIPLE 6

Look for Lessons

All experiences are opportunities for learning, and sickness is no exception. Anytime we face adversity, there are valuable insights to be gained. We learn about ourselves, and we learn about our priorities.

When we face serious illness, we must journey inward, reaching down to the core of our existence, searching for strength that we are not sure we possess.

An important part of your healing process is learning the lessons that you could have learned in no other way. As you complete your journey back to health, consider carefully what you've learned about yourself and your world. The following quotations can help.

We cannot learn without pain.

ARISTOTLE

There is no education like adversity.

BENJAMIN DISRAELI

Difficulty, my brethren,
is the nurse of greatness —
a harsh nurse, who roughly
rocks her foster-children
into strength.

William C. Bryant

I have always grown from
my problems and challenges,
from the things that don't
work out. That's when
I've really learned.

Carol Burnett

You are healed of a suffering
only by experiencing it
to the full.

Marcel Proust

There is nothing that the body suffers that the mind may not profit by.

GEORGE MEREDITH

In the darkest hour, the soul
is replenished and given
strength to endure.

Heart Warrior Chosa

One day the times of
struggle will strike you as
the most beautiful.

Sigmund Freud

Adversity introduces man
to himself.

Anonymous

The real voyage of discovery consists not in seeing new landscapes but in having new eyes.

MARCEL PROUST

In the depth of winter I learned that within me there lay an invincible summer.

ALBERT CAMUS

It is only because of problems that we grow mentally and spiritually.

M. Scott Peck

Deep suffering may well be called a baptism, the initiation into a new state.

George Eliot

Even a happy life cannot be without a measure of darkness, and the word "happiness" would lose its meaning if it were not balanced by sadness.

Carl Jung

Your pain is the breaking of the shell that encloses your understanding.

Khalil Gibran

That which does not kill me makes me stronger.

NIETZSCHE

Those things that hurt, instruct.

BEN FRANKLIN

Bad times have a scientific value. These are times that a good learner would not miss.
Ralph Waldo Emerson

Our trials are tests; they pave the way for a fuller life.
Jerome P. Fleishman

Sweet are the uses of adversity.
William Shakespeare

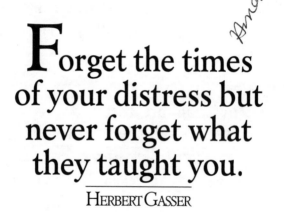

Forget the times
of your distress but
never forget what
they taught you.

HERBERT GASSER

PRINCIPLE 7

Be Thankful

When you're under the weather, it's easy to engage in self-pity. After all, you ask yourself, "What's there to be thankful for?"

The answer, if you stop to think about it, is "plenty." Even in times of poor health, you're the beneficiary of countless blessings; it's important to remember them.

So, if you're not feeling well — *especially* if you're not feeling well — still take time to stop and count your blessings. Because a thankful heart is also a healing heart.

The unthankful heart discovers no mercies, but the thankful heart finds, in every hour, some heavenly blessings.

HENRY WARD BEECHER

No duty is more urgent than that of returning thanks.

SAINT AMBROSE

Joy is what happens to us
when we allow ourselves to
recognize how good
things really are.

Marianne Williamson

Thanksgiving is a sure index
of spiritual health.

Maurice Dametz

Gratitude helps you to grow
and expand; gratitude brings
laughter into your life and
into the lives of all those
around you.

Eileen Caddy

Amen

Think of the beauty still left around you and give thanks.

ANNE FRANK

each of
piritual
ve got to
for it
heart.

n Breathnach

I thank you God for
this most amazing day....

e.e. cummings

Thank God every morning
when you get up that you
have something to do
which must be done,
whether you like it or not.

Charles Kingsley

Each day comes bearing its own gifts. Untie the ribbons.

RUTH ANN SCHABACKER

Think of the ills from which you are exempt.

JOSEPH JOUBERT

Gratitude is the sign
of noble souls.

Aesop

Gratitude to God makes
even a temporal blessing a
taste of heaven.

William Romaine

It is only with gratitude
that life becomes rich.

Dietrich Bonhoeffer

Ingratitude is always
    a form of weakness.

Goethe

When it comes to life,
    the critical thing is whether
you take things for granted or
    take them with gratitude.

G. K. Chesterton

Those who wish to
    sing always find a song.

Swedish Proverb

So much has been given me, I have no time to ponder over that which has been denied.

HELEN KELLER

What poison is to food,
   self-pity is to life.
                    Oliver C. Wilson

You can overcome
   anything if you don't
      bellyache.
                    Bernard Baruch

Sadness is almost never
   anything but a form
      of fatigue.
                    Andre Gide

Thanksgiving is never meant
to be shut up in a single day.

Robert Caspar Lintner

Gladly accept the gifts
of the present hour.

Horace

A thankful heart is not only
the greatest virtue, but the
parent of all other virtues.

Cicero

Life does not have to be perfect to be wonderful.

ANNETTE FUNICELLO

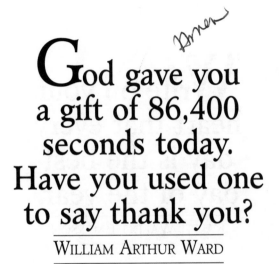

God gave you
a gift of 86,400
seconds today.
Have you used one
to say thank you?

WILLIAM ARTHUR WARD

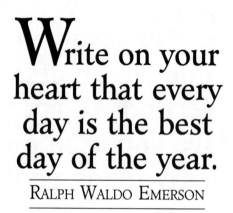

Write on your heart that every day is the best day of the year.

RALPH WALDO EMERSON

PRINCIPLE 8

Visualize Healing

As you complete the journey back to health, you'll find it helpful to visualize the healing process. As you develop a detailed vision of a new, improved, healthier you, that vision will put the self-fulfilling prophecy to work on your behalf.

The following quotations are intended to encourage the clear, unambiguous belief that your good health is just around the corner. That belief, firmly held, will help shape reality.

Persistent prophecy is a familiar way of assuring the event.

GEORGE R. GISSING

There is one thing which gives radiance to everything. It is the idea of something around the corner.

G. K. CHESTERTON

Before your dreams can come true, you have to have those dreams.

JOYCE BROTHERS

Vision is the art of seeing
things invisible.

Jonathan Swift

If you do not hope, you will
not find what is behind
your hopes.

St. Clement of Alexandria

Everything that is done in
the world is done by hope.

Martin Luther

Earth has no sorrow that
Heaven cannot heal.

Thomas More

When we can't dream
any longer, we die.

Emma Goldman

A man is not old until
regrets take the place
of his dreams.

John Barrymore

Nothing happens unless first a dream.

CARL SANDBURG

Keep your eyes on the stars and your feet on the ground.

Theodore Roosevelt

If one advances confidently in the direction of his dreams and endeavors to live the life he has imagined, he will meet a success unexpected in common hours.

HENRY DAVID THOREAU

Dreams never hurt anybody
who kept working right behind
the dream to make as much of
it come true as possible.

F. W. Woolworth

Talk about a dream
and try to make it true.

Bruce Springsteen

You should never agree to
surrender your dreams.

Jesse Jackson

Man is what he believes.

Anton Chekhov

Dream lofty dreams, and as you dream, so shall you become.

JOHN RUSKIN

The greatest discovery
of my generation is that
man can alter his life
simply by altering his
attitude of mind.

William James

A man is literally
what he thinks.

James Lane Allen

Hope is the physician of every ill.

IRISH PROVERB

Live from miracle to miracle.

ARTUR RUBINSTEIN

I take the position
that everything
in the universe
is trying to help
us regain health.

CARL SIMONTON

Sources

Quotations by Source

Get Well Soon...We Need You

Get Well Soon...We Need You

Kingsley, Charles 92
Kleiser, Granville 44
Levi, Peter 29
Lincoln, Abraham 23
Louden, William 52
Lowell, James Russell 35
Luther, Martin 107
Lyon, Mary 40
Mann, Horace 35
Marden, O. S. 29
McKay, David 68
Meredith, George 77
Michelangelo 64
More, Thomas 108
Niebuhr, Reinhold 72
Nietzsche 83
Osler, William 28
Ovid 46
Peale, Norman Vincent 27
Peck, M. Scott 81
Penn, William 63
Pindar 21
Powell, Colin 24
Proust, Marcel 76, 79
Proverbs 17:22 20
Reilly, Harold J. 42
Romaine, William 95
Roosevelt, Theodore 110

Sources

Get Well Soon...We Need You

About
DELANEY STREET PRESS

DELANEY STREET PRESS publishes a series of books designed to inspire and entertain readers of all ages. DELANEY STREET books are distributed by Walnut Grove Press. For more information, call 800-256-8584.

About the Author

Criswell Freeman is a Doctor of Clinical Psychology who lives, writes and works in Nashville, Tennessee. Dr. Freeman is also the author of *The Wisdom Series* published by Walnut Grove Press. *The Wisdom Series* is a collection of inspirational quotation books. In addition to his work as a writer, Freeman also hosts the nationally syndicated radio program *Wisdom Made in America*.